Six Flags Over Georgia at 50

Chadwick Miller

Copyright © 2017 Chadwick Miller
All rights reserved.
ISBN: 1544994303
ISBN-13: 978-1544994307

To Pajamas, Bumble, and Duffy for all your support

CONTENTS

	Preface	i
1	50 SFOG Facts	1
2	SFOG Timeline	21
3	SFOG Dictionary	49

Preface

Angus G. Wynne Jr visited Disneyland in Anaheim shortly after it opened in 1955 wanted to build a similar park in his home state of Texas. Six Flags Over Texas opened six years later, in 1961 and was an immediate success. This led to Wynne looking to expand and he settled on metro Atlanta. At the time, it was a rural outpost, with the land cheap and the whole region devoid of a large permanent amusement park. Six Flags Over Georgia opened in 1967, making Six Flags the first company with multiple parks. Disney would not open their second park, Walt Disney World in Florida, until 1971.

The name of the parks originated with the six flags that flew over the state of Texas. When it came time to expand to an additional park in Georgia, the task was to find six different countries that had ruled some portion of Georgia at any portion in the state's history. The six flags were Britain, France, Spain, United States, Confederate States, and the Georgia flag. These were a stretch as Georgia was never a sovereign nation as Texas was when it had its own flag flying over the state and later over the park. As the Six Flags parks have changed ownership groups and management companies, the historical aspect of the parks have declined. The parks still use some of the names to identify the different sections of the parks, but the themes have become more centered around Looney Tunes and DC Comics characters.

Now that Six Flags Over Georgia is celebrating its 50th Anniversary, I cannot help but reflect on how much the park meant to me and many people who grew up in metro Atlanta and all over the southeast. More accessible and much cheaper than Disney World, Six Flags Over Georgia was often the only park many children would grow up with. Researching this book was both a trip down memory lane and an opportunity to learn about rides long gone and the evolution of some of my favorites. I hope you enjoy the stroll down memory lane as much as I did.

50 SIX FLAGS OVER GEORGIA FACTS

Six Flags Over Georgia at 50 – Chadwick Miller

1 Six Flags Over Georgia opened on June 16th, 1967, with over 3,000 visitors on the first day.

2 Admission on opening day was $3.95 for adults and $.50 to park.

3 The original six areas of the park were Britain, Confederate, Spain, France, USA, and Georgia. These were the six flags represented in the original logo of the park.

4 The Rabun Gap train station is named after the area in the north Georgia mountains explorers would cross through on their way to the west.

5 The first costumed characters to walk around were Mr. Rabbit and Mr. Bear from the Tales of Okefenokee attraction.

6 There are four attractions from opening day that are still operating in their original locations: Dahlonega Mine Train, Six Flags Railroad, Crystal Pistol, and Sky Lift. The Hanson Cars moved from their original location to their current location in 1990.

7 The park originally had two entrances. The second (Back) entrance was closed in 1998 to make room for the Goldtown Racers (go-karts) the following year.

8 The two train engines on the Six Flags Railroad are named the Texas and the General, after the engines involved in the Great Locomotive Chase that originated in Kennesaw, GA.

9 The Captain Kangaroo show filmed on location at the park in 1976 complete with Mr. Green Jeans and Mr. Moose.

10 Local Atlanta area rescue personnel practice their white water rescue techniques in Thunder River as it is the best and safest rapid water simulation availabile.

11 The Dahlonega Mine Train is named after Dahlonega, GA, the home of the first gold rush in the United States in 1828.

12 The Mind Bender is billed as the world's first triple loop roller coaster, although the second loop is horizontal and riders do not actually go upside down.

13 Holiday in the Park has actually been at the park twice. Initially being celebrated 1989-1990 and then coming back on a more permanent basis in 2014.

14 When the Great American Scream Machine opened in 1973, riders were given a Red Badge of Courage for riding it. This promotion was repeated for the Georgia Cyclone when it opened in 1990.

15 The Riverview Carousel is a 1908 Philadelphia Toboggan Coasters Carousel and is one of the last five-abreast carousels known to still exist. It was added to the National Register of Historic Places on January 27, 1995.

16 The Lost Parents building in the shadow of Goliath is a replica of the first schoolhouse in Fulton County. This replica was built on the original site in 1957 and moved to the park a decade later. There is even a historical marker near the school house to mark its significance.

17 The current Log Flume attraction is not the original flume attraction. In 1968 the second flume was added and became the only flume when the original was removed before the park opened in 1991.

18 The Marthasville train station is named after Marthasville, GA, an earlier name for Atlanta and named after former Governor Wilson Lumpkin's daughter Martha.

19 When the Great American Scream Machine opened in 1973, it was the tallest (105 ft.), longest (3,450 ft.), and fastest (57 mph) roller coaster in the world.

20 Acrophobia uses rare-earth magnets to stop the attraction. This gives the ride a failsafe brake system and occupies a smaller footprint than electric braking systems.

21 Of the three Superman: Ultimate Flight rollercoasters in the United States, the one SFOG version is the only one with a dual loading platform and the only one with a tunnel for the track.

22 The wooden supports on the Dahlonega Mine Train are mostly ornamental. Over the years they have been replaced with steel supports and the wood is to maintain the theming of the ride.

23 Tales of Okefenokee was one of the original attractions, but went through a complete overhaul between 1967 and 1968. The Uncle Remus theming remained, but Sid and Marty Kroft did the redesign for year two of the attraction.

24 Without moving, the Mind Bender has been in three separate lands throughout its time at SFOG. It opened in 1978 in the USA section with a silver track. The following year, the area was rethemed to Jolly Rodger's Island and the track painted brown. In 1997, the area became the current Gotham City and the track was painted green.

25 SkyScreamer, the large swings attraction, is the tallest attraction in the park at 242 feet, besting Goliath by 42 feet.

26 The name Blue Hawk was selected by the public in a vote. Over 6,000 votes were cast and Blue Hawk was selected over American Eagle and Air Commander in 2016.

27 The SkyScreamer was renamed Patriots SkyScreamer for the opening weekend of 2017 due to a bet SFOG made with Six Flags New England over Super Bowl LI, where the New England Patriots beat the Atlanta Falcons.

28 As of 2017, the Georgia Scorcher, built in 1999, was the last stand-up roller coaster built in the world.

29 Superman: Ultimate Flight was the first rollercoaster in the world with a pretzel loop.

30 Monster Mansion is the world's largest animatronic-based family dark ride not based in a Disney park.

31 At the first offering of Holiday in the Park from 1989-1990, there was sledding on fake snow down one of the covered hills near the entrance of the park.

32 For the first eight years, there was a ride powered by a live mule. Initially called The Flying Jenny, it was renamed the Mule-Go-Round in 1971 until it closed in 1974.

33 Blue Hawk (when it was still Ninja) was in the 2015 film Vacation as the rollercoaster Velociraptor at Wally's World.

34 Looping Starship has been installed and removed from the park twice. Initially in 1985 it was installed in the spring and removed that fall, as it was on a rotation to visit other parks. Four years later, another version of the ride was installed in the same location and remained until 2005.

35 Thunder River, opening in 1982, is the oldest operating river rapids attraction in the world.

36 Joker's Funhouse is an updated paint scheme on the Spanish Fort that sits underneath the DC theming. The fort was originally modeled after the Castillo de San Marcos in St Augustine, FL.

37 Bufford Buzzard was a puppet who would tell jokes and insults to the crowds outside his cart along the walkway. He had a particular dislike for people from the neighboring Alabama.

38 Petsville was a petting zoo with live animals that was located near the Rabun Gap Train Station from 1967-1983.

39 Between the rotation, outward leaning harnesses, and floorless ride car, Acrophobia was the first free fall ride of its kind in the world.

40 In September 2009, metro Atlanta experienced torrential rain for days and SFOG and the surrounding area was almost completely under water, with the rollercoasters and taller attractions sticking up from the water. This happened at the beginning of the week and by the weekend, they were able to open on their regular schedule.

41 The shortest stay for a ride was just under three months in 1986. Mo-Mo the Monster was struck by lightning and temporarily removed for inspection and repair. The Great American Force, a spinning ride that used centrifugal force to stick riders up against a wall was brought in through the end of the season.

42 The original Looping Starship had the shuttle name Challenger painted on the side. When it returned, it was a generic shuttle with no reference to the Challenger tragedy in 1986.

43 Where Hurricane Harbor currently sits was a concert venue called the Southern Star Amphitheatre, from 1986-2013. Acts such as New Kids On the Block, Ray Charles, Lynyrd Skynyrd, and Sting played there over the years.

44 The original Spanish Fort had cannons that fired wax cannonballs at a target near the hill that now houses Splashwater Falls. Some of the wax cannonballs can still be found embedded in the hill.

45 In 1986, SFOG hosted the first regional Rubik's Cube-A-Thon. Everyone who solved it in under three minutes got a shirt and the fastest went on to the finals in New York.

46 In the early to mid-1980s, there was a Pac-Man Play Fort for kids, complete with a Pac-Man themed restaurant and a Pac-Man Magic Show where Pac-Man and Ms. Pac-Man were the magicians.

47 Log Flume 1 had a large animatronic villain who straddled the flume and sawed a log that always threatened to fall on riders below. Log Flume 2 had a large animatronic Paul Bunyan-like character that would chop at the logs as they went by.

48 Tales of Okefenokee was the dark ride that occupied the building that currently houses Monster Manor. Tales of Okefenokee lasted from 1967-1980 and told the Uncle Remus tales.

49 Throughout the 1980s and 1990s, there was an annual 10K road race in the spring called the "Six Miles at Six Flags."

50 SFOG hosted a roller coaster riding marathon on the Great American Scream Machine in 1998. The marathon lasted for 60 days and was called with three winners and each receiving a car. The contestants even slept on the platform at night.

SIX FLAGS OVER GEORGIA TIMELINE

Six Flags Over Georgia at 50 – Chadwick Miller

1961

- Six Flags Over Texas opens August 5

1965

- Great Southwest Corporation (parent company of Six Flags at the time) purchases 3,000 acres in metro Atlanta, GA

1967

*Six Flags Over Georgia opens
June 20, 1967*

- Animal Fair opens
- Astro Lift opens
- British Section opens
- Casa De Fritos opens
- Casa Loco opens
- Castillo DeSoto opens
- Confederate Section opens
- Crystal Pistol opens
- Dahlonega Mine Train opens
- Echo Well opens
- French Section opens
- Gaslight on the Green opens
- Georgia Section opens
- Hanson Cars opens
- Happy Motoring Freeway opens
- Jean Ribaults Adventure opens
- Krofft Puppet Theatre opens
- Lafayette's Shooting Gallery opens
- Log Jamboree opens
- Mini-Mine Train opens
- Mo-Mo The Monster opens
- Mule-Go-Round opens
- Petsville opens

- Six Flags Railroad opens
- Spanish Section opens
- Tales of the Okefenokee opens
- The French Trading Post opens
- U.S.A. Section opens

1968

- Casa Loco relocated outside Castillo DeSoto and renamed Casa Magnetica
- Chevy Show Cinema opens
- Dolphin Pool opens
- Horror Cave opens
- Lickskillet area opens
- Log Jamboree Flume 2 opens
- Naler's Plantation Restaurant opens
- Satellite Ride 1 relocates behind Ride 2
- Sky Buckets opens
- Spindletop opens
- Tales of the Okefenokee - all scenes changed
- Watermelon Waterloo opens
- Wheel Barrow opens

1969

- Sky Hook opens
- Yahoola Hooler opens

1970

- Wheel Burrow closes

1971

- Drunken Barrels opens
- Flying Jenny moves and is renamed the Mule-Go-Round

1972

- Riverview Carousel opens

1973

- Cotton States Exposition area opens
- Satellite Rides close
- Great American Scream Machine opens
- Yahoola Hooler renamed Mini-Mine Train

1974

- Mo-Mo the Monster opens
- Mule-Go-Round closes
- Phlying Phlurpus opens
- Sol Caliente opens
- The Krofft Brothers partnership with the park ends

1975

- American Pie Jamboree opens
- Animal Theatre opens
- Children's Theatre opens
- Ferris Wheel opens
- Gusano Contento (The Caterpillar) opens
- Happy Motoring Freeway closes
- Regata De Botes opens

1976

- Castillo DeSoto Cannons closes
- Great Gasp Parachute Ride opens
- Jumping Frijoles opens
- Krofft Theatre becomes Bicentennial Theatre
- Naler's Plantation Restaurant renamed

1977

- Buford Buzzard opens
- Halloweekends begins
- Phlying Phlurpus closes
- Plaza De Toros opens
- Sky Hook closes
- Wheelie opens

1978

- Mind Bender opens
- Mo-Mo The Monster moves to USA section

1979

- Bicentennial Theatre renamed Contemporary Theatre
- Gusano Contento (The Caterpillar) renamed Henry Hawk Happy Worm
- Highland Swings opens
- Spindle Top closes

1980

- Animal Theatre renamed Character Theatre
- Flying Dutchman opens
- Jolly Roger's Island opens
- Pizzas of Eight opens
- Ship Shape Theatre opens
- Tales of the Okefenokee closes

1981

- Jean Ribault's Adventure closes
- Monster Plantation opens
- The Astro Lifts closes

1982

- Casa De Fritos closes
- Echo Well closes
- Thunder River opens

1983

- Castillo DeSoto becomes the Pac-Man Playfort
- Dodge City Bumper Cars opens
- Freefall opens
- Mo-Mo The Monster moves to Cotton States Exposition
- Pac-Man Play Fort opens
- Petsville closes

1984

- Character Theatre renamed Shirt Tales Theatre
- Contemporary Theatre renamed Olympic Theatre
- Drunken Barrels closes
- Flying Turtles opens
- Hallmark's Shirt Tales characters arrive at the park
- The Great Six Flags Air Racer opens
- Pizzas of Eight renamed the Lighthouse Restaurant
- Regata De Botes closes

1985

- Carrot Patch opens
- Flying Turtles closes
- Horror Cave closes
- Loony Tunes characters arrive at the park
- Loony Tunes Land opens
- Looping Starship opens and closes at the end of the season
- Pac-Man Playfort renamed Yosemite Sam Playfort
- Olympic Theatre renamed The Looney Tunes Theatre
- Road Runner Runaround opens
- Sol Caliente renamed Elmer Fudd's Fewwis Wheel
- Tweety's Swings opens
- Wheelie moves to Lickskillet Section

1986

- Bill Clary's Magic Show opens
- Mo-Mo The Monster struck by lightning and temporarily closes
- Santa Maria opens
- Ship Shape Theatre becomes Graffiti's
- Shirt Tales leave
- Southern Star Amphitheatre opens
- Splashwater Falls opens
- The Great American Force opens and closes after a few months

1987

- Looney Tunes Theatre renamed the Showcase Theatre
- Mo-Mo The Monster reopens

1988

- Bill Clary's Magic Show replaced by the Loony Tunes Theatre (Kiddie) opens
- Mini-Mine Train closes
- Z-Force opens

1989

- Graffiti's renamed Illusion Theatre
- Holiday in the Park begins
- Looping Starship returns

1990

- Flying Tasmanian Devil Planes opens
- Georgia Cyclone opens
- Hanson Cars move to Carousel Hill
- Holiday in the Park ends
- Log Flume #1 closes

1991

- Mo-Mo The Monster closes
- Ragin' Rivers opens
- Z-Force closes

1992

- Illusion Theatre becomes Treasure Chest Arcade
- Ninja opens
- Road Runner's Convoy opens
- Tank Tag opens

1993

- Axis Arena opens with a Batman stunt show
- Dolphin Pool closes
- Henry Hawk Happy Worm closes

1994

- Elmer Fudd's Fewwis Wheel renamed Fiesta Wheel
- Flying Tasmanian Devil Planes renamed Little Aviator
- Loony Tunes Land becomes Bugs Bunny World
- Looney Tunes Theatre (Kiddie) renamed Bugs Bunny World Theatre
- Police Academy Live Action show is performed for one season
- Road Runner's Convoy renamed Convoy Grande
- Road Runner Runaround closes
- Showcase Theatre renamed Remember When Drive-In Theatre
- Tank Tag closes
- Toro Toro opens
- Treasure Chest Arcade closes
- Tweety's Swings renamed Swing Seville

1995

- Animal Action Show opens
- Viper opens
- Ultrazone indoor laser tag opens

1996

- Chevy Show renamed Plymouth Show
- Feerless Freep's Daredevil Dive
- Flying Dutchman closes
- Jolly Rodger's Island Section closes
- Ultrazone closes

1997

- Batman: The Ride opens
- Black Friar restaurant becomes Whistlin' Dixie
- Gotham City opens
- Highland Swings closes
- Mind Bender repainted green and themed to the Riddler

1998

- Back park entrance closes
- Buford Buzzard closes
- Park entrance remodeled into the Promenade
- Plymouth Show renamed U.S.A. Theater
- Ragin' Rivers closes
- Remember When Drive-In Theatre renamed Drive-In Theatre

1999

- Georgia Scorcher opens
- Goldtown Racers opens

2000

- Animal Action Show closes
- The Great Six Flags Air Racer closes

2001

- Acrophobia opens
- Déjà vu opens
- High Divers opens
- Log Jamboree #2 renamed Deer Park Plunge
- Tweety's Clubhouse opens
- Viper closes

2002

- Gaslight on the Green closes
- Metropolis Park opens
- Superman Ultimate Flight opens

2003

- U.S.A. Theater closes

2004

- Rockin' Tug opens
- Shake, Rattle and Roll opens
- Gotham City Crime Wave opens
- Up, Up & Away opens
- Wile E Coyote Canyon Blaster opens

2005

- Great Gasp closes
- Looping Starship closes
- Skull Island opens
- Whistlin' Dixie restaurant becomes Panda Express

2006

- Deer Park Plunge renamed Log Jamboree
- Free Fall closes
- Goliath opens

2007

- Déjà vu closes
- High Divers closes
- Tondee's Tavern closes

2008

- Back to the Beach show opens
- Confederate Section renamed Peachtree Square
- Thomas Town opens

2009

- Back to the Beach show closes
- Drive-In Theatre closes
- Monster Plantation renamed Monster Mansion

2010

- Fearless Freep's Dare Devil Dive is renamed Sky Coaster
- Shake Rattle and Roll closes

2011

- Dare Devil Dive opens
- Thomas Town becomes Whistlestop Park
- Tondee's Tavern restaurant becomes Johnny Rockets

2012

- Wheelie closes

2013

- SkyScreamer opens
- Skull Island closes
- Southern Star Amphitheater closes

2014

- Bonzai Pipelines opens
- Calypso Bay opens
- Holiday in the Park begins again
- Hurricane Harbor opens
- Paradise Island opens
- Tsunami Surge opens

2015

- Carrot Patch closes
- Harley Quinn Spinsanity opens
- Little Aviator closes
- Spanish Section closes
- The Joker: Chaos Coaster opens
- Toro Toro closes
- Whistlestop Park closes

2016

- Batman Batcopters opens
- Bugs Bunny World becomes Bugs Bunny Boomtown
- Convoy Grande renamed Acme Trucking Co
- Cotton States Exposition Section closes
- Daffy Duck's Bucket Blasters opens
- DC Super Friends area added
- Dodge City Bumper Cars closes
- Fiesta Wheel renamed Yosemite Sam's Wacky Wagons
- Little Aviator closes
- Ninja is repainted blue and gray and becomes Blue Hawk
- Santa Maria renamed Bugs Bunny High Sea Adventure
- Speedy Gonzales Speed Boats opens
- Superman: Tower of Power opens
- Swing Seville closes
- Toro Toro closes
- Wile E. Coyote Canyon Blaster renamed The Joker Funhouse Coaster
- Wonder Woman Flight School opens
- Yosemite Sam Playfort renamed Joker Funhouse

2017

- Blue Hawk and Great American Scream Machine are now part of Lickskillet
- Cotton States Exposition area is rethemed to Metropolis
- Justice League: Battle for Metropolis opens
- Georgia Cyclone closes

2018

- Twisted Cyclone opens

2019

- Pandemonium opens

Six Flags Over Georgia at 50 – Chadwick Miller

SIX FLAGS OVER GEORGIA DICTIONARY

Acme Trucking Co
2016-Current
Small tractor-trailer themed attraction designed for children. The trucks are attached so they roll around the track in a single-file line. Each semi holds two riders. This attraction originally opened in 1992 as Road Runner's Convoy, renamed Convoy Grande in 1994 and was renamed Acme Trucking Co in 2016.

Acrophobia
2001-Current
200 foot tall free-fall tower ride. As it raises riders up, it rotates around the pole once and upon reaching the top tilts riders 15 degrees out, so they are looking down at the ground. This ride opened in 2001, using the same tower at The Great Six Flags Air Racer.

American Pie Jamboree
1975-1978
American themed show for the U.S.A.'s Bicentennial Celebration and was the last show in the Kroft Theatre before it was renamed the Bicentennial Theatre in 1976.

Animal Action Show
1995-2000
Live action animal show, located on the covered dolphin pool between the French and Spanish Sections.

Animal Theatre
1975-1979
Outside theatre in the kiddie section that had live animals in a caged in stage as stars of the show Was renamed the Character Theatre in 1980.

Astro Lift
1967-1981
One of the original attractions in the park, it was cable cars that connect the Confederate Section to the U.S.A. Section. This was the first of two cable car rides that took guests all over the park, with the second one, the Sky Buckets, opening in 1968 and remaining open to this day. The Astro Lift was closed to make way for the Free Fall in the U.S.A. Section.

Axis Arena
1993-Current
Arena in Gotham City that opened with a Batman themed stunt show. After the Batman show closed, the arena is used for special events and concerts. The theme of Axis Arena is based on Axis Chemical Plant, where Jack Napier fell into a vat of chemicals and became the Joker.

B

Back to the Beach Show
2008-2009
After the return of the high divers, the pool was covered again and Back to the Beach was performed on the covered pool for two seasons. The pool was located between the French and Spanish Sections.

Batman: The Ride
1997-Current
Steel roller coaster with cars that hang from the track instead of riding on top like traditional coasters. Riders sit in the car, but the floor drops away before leaving the station, allowing riders' feet to dangle and swing throughout the ride. Opening in 1997, it has a top speed of 50 mph and is 105 feet tall.

Batman Batcopters
2016-Current
Spinning kiddie ride with ride vehicles shaped like helicopters with controls that allow riders to control the height of their Batcopter as they spin.

Bicentennial Theatre
1976-1978
The renamed and redecorated Kroft Theatre for the U.S.A.'s Bicentennial Celebration. The show that occupied the Bicentennial Theatre was American Pie Jamboree. At the conclusion of the celebration, it was renamed the Contemporary Theatre in 1979.

Bill Clary's Magic Show
1986-1987
Magic show that occupied the outdoor theatre in the kiddie section. Replaced by the Looney Tunes Theatre in 1988.

Black Friar Restaurant
1967-1996
One of the original restaurants in the park, it was located in the Confederate Section. It was changed to Whistlin' Dixie in 1997 and then became a Panda Express in 2005.

Blue Hawk
2016-Current
Steel roller coaster over the water next to the Great American Scream Machine. It opened in 1992 as the Ninja. In 2016 it was painted blue, received new cars and was renamed Blue Hawk. It has a top speed of 52 mph and is 122 feet tall.

Bonzai Pipelines
2014-Current
Trio of water slides in Hurricane Harbor that opened in 2014.

British Section
1967-Current
One of the six original sections of the park. It was immediately to the right upon entering the main gate, with shops and stores with British sounding names. After the Hanson Cars moved and were replaced by the Georgia Cyclone, this area began to lose its identity.

Bugs Bunny Boomtown
2016-Current
Children's area that houses many Looney Tunes rides for families and kids. Initially opened as Looney Tunes Land in 1985, then renamed Bugs Bunny World in 1994, finally becoming the current Bugs Bunny Boomtown in 2016.

Bugs Bunny High Sea Adventure
2016-Current
Two seater boats that raise up and swing kids around in a small circle. Similar to other swing rides throughout the park, just on a smaller scale and was renamed Bugs Bunny High Sea Adventure in 2016. Originally opened as the Santa Maria in 1986.

Bugs Bunny World
1994-2015
Looney Tunes themed kid area. Many of the existing rides were renamed and rethemed to fit in with Bugs Bunny and his friends. This area was renamed Bugs Bunny Boomtown in 2016.

Bugs Bunny World Theatre
1994-2015
Outdoor theatre in the kiddie section. The Looney Tunes Theatre was renamed the Bugs Bunny World Theatre when the entire kiddie area was renamed Bugs Bunny World.

Buford Buzzard
1977-1998
Buzzard puppet who resided in a caravan cart parked on the walkway of the park. The puppet would tell jokes and insult his audience, especially the ones from Alabama. Created and originally performed by Alan Kline.

Calypso Bay
2014-Current
Wave pool containing 38,000 gallons of water located in Hurricane Harbor, opening in 2014.

Carrot Patch
1985-2015
Room full of giant carrots hanging from the ceiling for kids to run around through, pushing the carrots and making them swing. Located in the Yosemite Sam Playfort, these carrots were basically carrot-shaped soft punching bags.

Casa de Fritos
1967-1982
One of the original restaurants in the park, located inside the Castillo DeSoto in the Spanish Section of the park. While it sounds like the restaurant should have featured corn chips, its focus was "authentic" Mexican food, consisting of tacos, burritos, and a taco dog.

Casa Loco
1967-1967
One of the original attractions of the park, located in Castillo DeSoto in the Spanish Section. The main attraction was a room designed at an angle, complete with a sloping floor where park employees would do tricks and demonstrations to show the effects of gravity to the guests. The attraction lasted one year inside the fort and moved outside the following year and was renamed Casa Magnetica.

Casa Magnetica
1968-1983
Once the Casa Loco moved outside Castillo DeSoto, it was renamed Casa Magnetica. The main attraction was still a room designed at an angle, complete with a sloping floor where park employees would do tricks and demonstrations to show the effects of gravity to the guests.

Castillo DeSoto
1967-1982
Former centerpiece of the Spanish Section of the park. The fort was designed after the Spanish fort Castillo de San Marcos in St Augustine, FL. The SFOG version had two stories and many different rooms and areas that over the years housed cannons, a poster shop, Casa de Fritos, Casa Loco, and the Horror Cave to name a few.

Castillo DeSoto Cannons
1967-1976
Cannons located on the top level of the Castillo DeSoto that fired wax cannonballs at targets located on the hill that currently houses Splashwater Falls.

Character Theatre
1980-1983
Outdoor theatre in the kiddie section. Originally the Animal Theatre, it became the Shirt Talcs theatre in 1984-1985.

Chevy Show
1968-1995
Theater with a screen that went 180 degrees around the audience and arched overhead as well. It would show point of view films to make viewers feel like they were actually participating in the films (riding roller coasters, driving speeding cars, etc.), not just watching a movie. It was located in the U.S.A. Section and when the sponsorship by Chevrolet ended, it was sponsored by Plymouth and renamed the Plymouth Show for two years.

Confederate Section
1967-2007
One of the original sections of the park around the Crystal Pistol. Renamed as Peachtree Square in 2008. By then, most of the antebellum themes had been switched over to modern naming and theming.

Contemporary Theatre
1979-1983
Located in the U.S.A. Section, the Contemporary Theatre was a renamed and redecorated Bicentennial Theatre. The Contemporary Theatre was itself renamed the Olympic Theatre in 1984.

Convoy Grande
1994-2015
Small tractor-trailer themed attraction designed for children. The trucks are attached so they roll around the track in a single-file line. Each semi holds two riders. This attraction originally opened in 1992 as Road Runner's Convoy, renamed Convoy Grande in 1994 and again renamed Acme Trucking Co in 2016.

Cotton States Exposition Section
1973-2016
World fair themed area of the park that held the Great American Scream Machine when it opened. Also contained many midway-style games and attractions. After the addition of Superman: Ultimate Flight, it began the slow loss of area for the Cotton States Exposition. After Dodge City Bumper Cars was closed for the Justice League: Battle for Metropolis, the Cotton States Exposition was split up with half the area becoming Metropolis Park and the other half becoming park of the Lickskillet Section.

Crystal Pistol
1967-Current
Performance venue with antebellum theming. Shows usually include a combination of current and classic popular songs performed by local talent. This venue was one of the original attractions in the park.

Daffy Duck's Bucket Blasters
2016-Current
Buckets that rotate around a center island with up to four children per bucket. Each bucket is equipped with water guns that allow riders to shoot other buckets and guests who get too close to the viewing fence.

Dahlonega Mine Train
1967-Current
Steel roller coaster, one of the original attractions in the park. Themed after the mining town of Dahlonega in north Georgia, home of the nation's first gold rush. It has wooden supports and a track, designed to resemble the mining carts used to mine for gold. It has a top speed of 29 mph and is 37 feet tall. This coaster opened up much longer than it currently sits as the track was shortened in 1986 for the construction of Splashwater Falls.

Dare Devil Dive
2011-Current
Steel roller coaster that simulates the flight pattern of a jet fighter. The coaster initially goes almost straight up then drops almost straight down before quietly mimicking a fighter jet. During certain periods of the year, riders wear virtual reality goggles so riders could shoot goblins as they flew through a city. This coaster has a top speed of 52 mph, is 95 feet tall, and opened in 2011.

DC Super Friends Area
2016-Current
DC Comics themed area for smaller guests. Located near the center of the park, across the walkway from Monster Mansion.

Deer Park Plunge
2001-2005
Log flume ride which is actually the second log ride in the park. The first Log Jamboree opened in 1967 and was so popular, the current one was opened the following year, in 1968. Log Jamboree #1 was torn down in 1991 to make way for Ragin' Rivers and Log Jamboree #2 became the only Log Jamboree. In 2001, it was renamed Deer Park Plunge and in 2006, its name was reversed back to Log Jamboree.

Déjà Vu
2001-2007
Steel looping roller coaster that would launch from the platform and then go through the blue and green looping track before then going back through the same track backwards. It had a top speed of 65.6 mph and was 194 feet tall.

Dodge City Bumper Cars
1983-2016
Traditional bumper car attraction, with single and two seater cars with metal poles connecting them to the metal grate on the ceiling providing the power. The track had a concrete island, designed to give the track an actual track feel, but you were free to drive in any direction, as long as you didn't mind bumping in to everyone.

Dolphin Pool
1968-1993
Dolphin pool located on the border of the Spanish and French Sections. Kathy Bennet was the original trainer of Skipper and Dolly, the pair of bottle nosed dolphins. After Kathy moved on, the dolphins had a rotating cast of trainers and then shared their pool with a high diving show. This combination lasted until the pool was covered up for a Police Academy comedy show.

Drive-In Theatre
1998-2009
Located in the U.S.A. Section, the Drive-In Theatre was a renamed Remember When Drive-In Theatre. The Drive-In Theatre was the last theatre name for the building that began as the Kroft Puppet Theatre and was torn down in 2010 for the construction of Dare Devil Dive.

Drunken Barrels
1971-1984
Spinning, tea cup style ride with barrel shaped spinning ride vehicles that would spin around a plate, with the riders controlling how fast their individual barrel would spin. This attraction was in the Lickskillet Section and replaced the Wheel Burrow.

Echo Well
1967-1982
Well just outside the Spanish Fort that had a recording mechanism in the bottom that would instantly play back whatever someone would shout into the well.

Elmer Fudd's Fiesta Wheel
1985-1993
Originally opened as Sol Caliente in 1974. It was renamed the Elmer Fudd's Fewwis Wheel in 1985 and renamed the Fiesta Wheel in 1994. It was again renamed and rethemed in 2016 as Yosemite Sam's Wacky Wagons.

F

Feerless Freep's Daredevil Dive
1996-2009
Large swing ride that includes an additional cost in addition to park admission. 180 foot arch with a swinging platform for guests to lie down suspended within the arch. The platform is pulled back and riders swing out over the same lake that houses the Great American Scream Machine. It opened in 1996 as Feerless Freep's Daredevil Dive but changed its name in 2010 to Sky Coaster when the Dare Devil Dive roller coaster opened.

Fiesta Wheel
1994.-2015
Miniature Ferris Wheel for little riders with a statue of Speedy Gonzalez out front. Originally opened as Sol Caliente in 1974. It was renamed the Elmer Fudd's Fewwis Wheel in 1985 and renamed the Fiesta Wheel in 1994. It was again renamed and rethemed in 2016 as Yosemite Sam's Wacky Wagons.

Flying Dutchman
1980-1996
Pirate themed boat that would swing back and forth, with the riders on the ends getting high enough to be looking down at the ground. The ship would never loop completely over, just give the impression that it was close.

Flying Jenny
1967-1970
Merry-Go-Round with riders suspended in gondolas and the ride was powered by a mule named Jenny. This ride was renamed Mule-Go-Round in 1971.

Flying Tasmanian Devil Planes
1990-1993
Biplane ride where kids could control the height of the planes as they rotated around a central hub. Opened in 1990 as Flying Tasmanian Devil Planes and renamed Little Aviator in 1994.

Flying Turtles
1984-1985
Little seats with handlebars and wheels that kids would ride around an enclosed track. These were pinched fingers just waiting to happen and only lasted two years.

Free Fall
1983-2006
Tower ride that would raise guests to the top of the tower in a four-seater car and then drop them. The ride would get to the bottom and then the car would tilt so guests were on their backs before sliding back down into the upright position in the station. This ride was in the U.S.A. Section and was removed for the construction of Goliath.

Fright Fest
1977-Current
Annual Halloween celebration which began as Halloweekends in 1977, its one of the biggest Halloween celebrations in the South. Zombies, chainsaw-wielding clowns, and many other creatures of nightmares roam the park scaring guests. Multiple haunted houses are available for an up charge in addition to the Halloween themed shows and decorations included with admission throughout the park.

French Section
1967-Current
One of the original sections of the park. The main attraction when the section opened was Jean Ribault's Adventure, which later became Thunder River. This section has evolved over time, losing the water ride but gaining Monster Mansion. At this point, it is French in name only.

Gaslight on the Green
1967-2002
Located in the French Section, it was one of the original restaurants in the park. While it was the main restaurant in the French Section, the food offered was far from French, it was your traditional park faire. Gaslight on the Green was replaced by El Jalapeno Jr. in 2002.

Georgia Cyclone
1990-2017
Wooden roller coaster inspired by the Coney Island Cyclone. The Georgia version is a mirror version of the original with minor changes. It has a top speed of 50 mph and is 95 feet tall.

Georgia Scorcher
1999-Current
Stand-up roller coaster in the Georgia Section. It has a top speed of 54 mph and is 107 feet tall.

Georgia Section
1967-Current
One of the original sections of the park, located to left after entering the park. It initially contained just the Log Jamboree, but over the years has had both Log Flumes, Ragin' Rivers, and currently Georgia Scorcher and Long Jamboree. The Georgia Cyclone is not in the Georgia Section.

Goldtown Racers
1999-Current
Go-karts in the rear of the park where the second entrance originally was located. This is attraction is an additional cost and not included with admission.

Goliath
2006-Current
Steel roller coaster that has a max height of 200 ft. and tops out at 70 mph. Its orange track can be seen long before the rest of the park and the track actually takes riders outside the park.

Gotham City
1997-Current
DC Comics themed area that opened in 1997, replacing the Jolly Roger's Island area. The main focus of this area is on Batman and his adversaries; the Riddler, the Joker, and Harley Quinn. A replica of the Batmobile from *Batman* and *Batman Returns* is in the hub as guests walk into the area.

Gotham City Crime Wave
2004-Current
Swings that hang around a center pole decorated with pictures of DC Comics villains such as Harley Quinn and Mr. Freeze. As the ride spins and swings the riders, it also tilts, giving an added thrill to the traditional swing ride.

Graffiti's
1986-1988
Theatre in the Jolly Rodger's Island Section. Preceded by the Ship Shape Theatre and followed by the Illusion Theatre.

Great American Scream Machine
1973-Current
Park's original wooden roller coaster. When this coaster was built, it reignited a renaissance of wooden coaster building at amusement parks around the world. Over the years, the cars have been turned around and riders are able to ride the coaster backwards. It has a top speed of 57 mph and is 105 feet tall.

Great Gasp
1976-2005
Parachute ride that was the icon of the park during its lifetime at the park. Riders would sit on a bench that would be raised up to the top of the tower and then float gently down to the ground. The tower was often the first thing visitors would see from the interstate as they approached the park. The Great Gasp was located in the U.S.A. Section and removed for the construction of Goliath.

Gusano Contento (The Caterpillar)
1975-1978
Kiddie ride that was a bouncing caterpillar that rolled around in a circle and lightly bounced the little riders. Early on, it had a sombrero on to fit in with the theming of the area. Once it was renamed the Henry Hawk Happy Worm, it was hatless.

Hanson Cars
1967-Current
Antique cars that are guided along a rail in the ground, but guests can control the speed and steering (to an extent). This ride opened in 1967 in the British Section, where the Georgia Cyclone currently sits. The Cyclone still uses the old Hanson Cars queue building for guests to wait. The original track wound through the countryside, over a bridge and through a barn. It was moved to carousel hill in 1990 to make way for the Cyclone and has ringed the carousel ever since.

Happy Motoring Freeway
1967-1975
One of the original attractions of the park, located in the U.S.A. Section. The ride consisted of gas powered miniature cars that guests would drive around a track that had a guide rail to keep the cars on track. The track itself was designed to look like the interstate highways that had begun crisscrossing the country a decade earlier. The ride was sponsored by Humble Oil and even had company billboards to make the interstates feel authentic. During Humble's sponsorship, the name of the gas company was changed to Exxon in 1971 for a more nationwide appeal and the signage on the buildings and billboards was changed to reflect this rebranding. This attraction was removed for construction of the Great Gasp.

Harley Quinn Spinsanity
2015-Current
Tilt-A-Whirl style ride with seven cars that spin around a central point as the ground below them undulates up and down, causing the cars to spin and bob up and down. Harley Quinn is a supervillain from the Batman comics, often associated with the Joker.

Henry Hawk Happy Worm
1979-1993
Kiddie ride that was a bouncing caterpillar that rolled around in a circle and lightly bounced the little riders. Originally opened as Gusano Contento (The Caterpillar) and was renamed the Henry Hawk Happy Worm in 1979.

High Divers
2001-2007
After sharing the dolphin pool with the dolphins the first time around, the high divers returned to the pool and were the only performers. The pool was located between the French and Spanish Sections.

Highland Swings
1979-1997
Swing ride that was located in the British Section and was removed for the construction of the Georgia Cyclone. Relatively tame compared to the current swing rides in the park, the Highland Swings did not go too far off the ground and the ride itself did not tilt or rock back and forth.

Holiday in the Park
2014-Current
Annual Christmas celebration throughout the park. The park is decorated for the holidays, there are special Christmas and winter themed shows and the train has a winter theme to it. It initially ran from 1989-1990 and was brought back on an annual basis in 2014.

Horror Cave
1968-1985
Haunted house that was located in the Castillo De Soto in the Spanish Section. Guests would enter through a monster's mouth and walk through a variety of creepy or scary scenes such as a mad scientist's laboratory, bridge over a pit that contained a man-eating spider, creatures in a murky lagoon, and man standing over a decapitated woman.

Hurricane Harbor
2014-Current
Water park in the rear of the park that replaced the Southern Star Amphitheater. This attraction has a combination of slides, wave pool, and children's area.

Illusion Theatre
1989-1991
The last theatre in the Jolly Rodger's Island Section. Preceded by Graffiti's and was turned into the Treasure Chest Arcade in 1992.

J

Jean Ribault's Adventure
1967-1981
Located in the French Section, this slow moving riverboat ride told the tale of French explorer Jean Ribault. While Ribault never settled Georgia, having colonized portions of South Carolina and Florida, the ride used animatronic figures and scenes to show some of the trials and tribulations the early explorers and colonizers faced in the Southeast United States. This ride was removed and the channel the boats floated through was redesigned to become Thunder River.

Jolly Rodger's Island Section
1980-1996
Pirate themed section of the park that housed the Flying Dutchman and Mind Bender along with many pirate themed restaurants and shops. This area became Gotham City with the arrival of Batman: The Ride and the Axis Arena.

Jumping Frijoles (Mexican Jumping Beans)
1976-1984
Circular flat ride with ride vehicles shaped like a giant bean wearing a sombrero that would raise and lower as they would rotate, giving the impression of jumping.

Justice League: Battle for Metropolis
2017-Current
The first interactive dark ride in SFOG, ride vehicles will be equipped with laser guns they are able to fire at the 3D screens and interactive visuals as they ride through the attraction. Guests fight Lex Luthor and the Joker to rescue Green Lantern, The Flash, Wonder Woman, and Supergirl and save Metropolis.

Kroft Puppet Theatre
1967-1975
One of the original attractions in the park, it was a theatre with a puppet show deigned by Sid and Marty Kroft in the U.S.A. Section of the park.

Lickskillet Section
1968-Current
Area of the park initially themed to look like a rural town in Georgia that was located at the intersection I20 and I285 just a few miles east of the park. The area was renamed from Lickskillet to Adamsville in 1906.

Little Aviator
1994-2015
Biplane ride where kids could control the height of the planes as they rotated around a central hub. Opened in 1990 as Flying Tasmanian Devil Planes and renamed Little Aviator in 1994.

Log Jamboree
1968-Current
Log flume ride which is actually the second log ride in the park. The first Log Jamboree opened in 1967 and was so popular, the current one was opened the following year, in 1968. Log Jamboree #1was torn down in 1991 to make way for Ragin' Rivers and Log Jamboree #2 became the only Log Jamboree. In 2001, it was renamed Deer Park Plunge and in 2006, its name was reversed back to Log Jamboree.

Long Jamboree #1
1967-1990
Log flume ride that was one of the original rides in the park, located in the Georgia Section, and was so popular, a second flume was added a year later. The log flume ride was inspired by the logging industry's practice of sending trees down streams and rivers as a much easier and faster mode of transporting logs in the early days of logging. On this version, guests would ride in log shaped vehicles through a watery path that wound through the woods of SFOG. The original flume was removed to make way for Ragin' Rivers, but the second flume remains.

Looney Tunes Adventure Camp
2010-Current
Large playground area in the kid section of the park with slides and rope bridges. Opened in 2010.

Looney Tunes Land
1985-1993
Bugs Bunny and friends themed kids' area, taking over part of the Spanish Section and the Pac-Man Playfort and retheming as for Looney Tunes.

Looney Tunes Theatre (U.S.A. Section)
1985-1986
Located in the U.S.A. Section, the Looney Tunes Theatre was a renamed and redecorated Olympic Theatre. The Looney Tunes Theatre was itself renamed the Showcase Theatre in 1987

Looney Tunes Theatre (Kiddie)
1988-1993
Outdoor theatre in the kiddie section. When Looney Tunes characters moved into the park, it was renamed the Looney Tunes Theatre and began having shows featuring Bugs Bunny and friends.

Looping Starship
1985-1985
1989-2005

The Looping Starship is unique in that the ride made two stops at SFOG. The first was for a scheduled yearlong stop that was part of tour the ride was making around American amusement parks. The return of the Looping Starship was not a true return in that it wasn't the exact same ride that was there in 1985, just the same model. The ride itself was a space shuttle that would rock back and forth, with the arcs getting higher and higher until it made a complete loop. The ride would make a few complete loops and then slowly rock back to a stop. The ride was located in the U.S.A. Section and was removed for the construction of Goliath.

Metropolis Park
2002-Current
DC Comics themed area with the Superman: Ultimate Flight coaster and Justice League: Battle for Metropolis. As opposed to the Gotham City area, Metropolis Park is more focused on Superman and his villains.

Mind Bender
1978-Current
First triple loop roller coaster and despite being almost 40 years old, is still regarded as one of the top roller coasters in the park. It has a top speed of 50 mph and is 80 feet tall.

Mini Mine Train
1973-1988
Steel junior coaster that was built for the smaller riders to enjoy as their more adult family members enjoyed the Dahlonega Mine Train. The Mini Mine Train track looped through the track for the Dahlonega Mine Train and shared the same early gold rush theming. It originally opened as the Yahoola Hooler in 1969 and was renamed the Mini Mine Train in 1973. It had a top speed of 20 mph and was 20 feet tall.

Mo-Mo the Monster
1974-1991
Spinning octopus style ride with a central hub and arms that came off and on the end of each arm was a hand with four ride vehicles. The ride vehicles would individually spin as the hand would spin as the arms rotated around the hub. In 1978, the attraction was relocated to the former site of the Sky Hook in the U.S.A. Section. The ride was struck by lightning in 1986 and removed for repair and inspection, returning in 1987.

Monster Mansion
2009-Current
Dark ride where riders float through a flooded mansion with a variety of scenes of friendly monsters having a picnic. The boats then go through the marsh, filled with scary monsters before ending back with the friendly monsters. From 1981 – 2008, this ride was known as Monster Plantation before a refurbishment and addition of the photo service at the beginning and the addition of a few new monsters.

Monster Plantation
1981-2008
Dark ride where riders float through a flooded mansion with a variety of scenes of friendly monsters having a picnic. The boats then go through the marsh, filled with scary monsters before ending back with the friendly monsters. From 1981 – 2008, this ride was known as Monster Plantation before a refurbishment and addition of the photo service at the beginning and the addition of a few new monsters.

Mule-Go-Round
1971-1974
Merry-Go-Round with riders suspended in gondolas and the ride was powered by a mule named Jenny. This ride originally opened as Flying Jenny in 1967 and was renamed Mule-Go-Round in 1971.

Naler's Plantation Restaurant
1968-1975
Located in the Confederate Section, Naler's Plantation replaced Lacy Restaurant, which was one of the original restaurants in the park. The location in SFOG was part of the Naler's Plantation of fried chicken restaurant chain based in Texas and there were locations in many of the original Six Flags parks. The Naler name was removed in 1976 and it remained the Plantation House, serving fried chicken until it changed names in 2008.

Ninja
1992-2015
Steel roller coaster over the water next to the Great American Scream Machine. It opened in 1992 as the Ninja with a red and black paint scheme. In 2016 it was painted blue, received new cars and was renamed Blue Hawk. It had a top speed of 52 mph and was 122 feet tall.

Olympic Theatre
1984-1984
Theatre in the U.S.A. Section, it was only named the Olympic Theatre for one season, in between being called the Contemporary Theatre and the Looney Tunes Theatre.

P

Pac-Man Playfort
1983-1984

Pac-Man, the king of classic arcade games, was a walk around character at SFOG for two years and took over the Castillo DeSoto, renaming and retheming it as Pac-Man Playfort. The playfort consisted of Pipeline Crawl, Boppity Bags, Walk On Water, Ball Bath, and King of the Mountain. Pac-Man and his Playfort lasted at SFOG for only two years, being replaced by the Looney Tunes characters and the playfort becoming the Yosemite Sam Playfort.

Pandimonium
2019-Current
Oversized pendulum ride that seats 40 people, travels at 50 mph and goes up to 147 feet in the air. The pendulum swings back and forth while rotating the riders clockwise as well.

Paradise Island
2014-Current
Water playground located in Hurricane Harbor, containing water cannons, multiple water slides, a giant bucket that tips over when it fills up, and many other children play areas.

Peachtree Square Section
2008-Current
Replaced the Confederate Section when Monster Plantation was renamed Monster Mansion. Many of the restaurants and shops in this area had their names changed to more generic theme park names as well.

Petsville
1967-1983
Petting zoo with the traditional barnyard animals. It also included a seal pool with an underwater viewing window so guests could watch them swim.

Phlying Phlurpus
1974-1977
Spinning ride whose ride vehicles had a giant fin on the front that riders could use to lightly steer the vehicle as it spun around. This was a larger, adult version, of Wonder Woman Flight School. Also went by the names: Phenominal Phlying Phlurpus (1974), Captain Phileas Fogg's Fabulous Electric Fliers (1975), and Electric Fliers (1976-77).

Pizzas of Eight
1980-1983
Pirate themed restaurant located in the newly opened Jolly Rodger's Island. This restaurant had a lighthouse on top and served pizza. Renamed the Lighthouse Restaurant in 1984.

Plaza De Toros (The Matador Ride)
1977-1993
Circular flat kiddie ride with ride vehicles shaped like bulls that rotated around a central hub. Located just outside the Castillo DeSoto.

Plymouth Show
1996-1997
Originally named the Chevy Show, when the sponsorship by Chevrolet ended, it was sponsored by Plymouth for two years. Theater with a screen that went 180 degrees around the audience and arched overhead as well. It would show point of view films to make viewers feel like they were actually participating in the films (riding roller coasters, driving speeding cars, etc.), not just watching a movie. It was located in the U.S.A. Section and when the sponsorship by Plymouth ended, it was renamed the U.S.A. Theater in 1998.

Promenade
1967-Current
Entrance to the park. Currently is lined with shops and restaurants giving it an open air shopping mall feel. Originally, it was lined with Greek columns and the six flags that were part of the logo.

Police Academy Live Action
1994-1994
Comedy show based on the Police Academy series of films, located on the covered dolphin pool between the French and Spanish Sections.

R

Ragin' Rivers
1991-1998
A pair of water slide attractions that sat where Georgia Scorcher now stands. There were a pair of twisting enclosed tubes and a pair of open straight slides. These slides were done in pairs so that riders would be able race each other down and add another layer of entertainment to the attraction.

Regata De Botes
1975-1984
Circular kiddie boat ride, similar to the current Speedy Gonzalez Speed Boats.

Remember When Drive-In Theatre
1994-1997
Located in the U.S.A. Section, the Remember When Drive-In Theatre was a renamed Showcase Theatre. In 1998, the name was shortened to Drive-In Theatre.

Riverview Carousel
1972-Current
Five abreast carousel that was originally built in 1908 for the Riverview Park in Chicago, IL. When that park closed in 1967, the carousel was sold to SFOG and opened in 1972. It was added to the National Register of Historic Places in 1995.

Road Runner's Convoy
1992-1993
Small tractor-trailer themed attraction designed for children. The trucks are attached so they roll around the track in a single-file line. Each semi holds two riders. This attraction originally opened in 1992 as Road Runner's Convoy, renamed Convoy Grande in 1994 and again renamed Acme Trucking Co in 2016.

Road Runner Runaround
1985-1993
Looney Tunes themed car ride for kids. Road Runner was the fastest of the Looney Tunes characters and was a natural fit for a car attraction.

Rockin' Tug
2004-Current
Tugboat that slowly spins as it slides back and forth to simulate rocking on the water. This kiddie ride opened in 2004.

S

Santa Maria
1986-2015
Two seater boats that raise up and swing kids around in a small circle. Similar to other swing rides throughout the park, just on a smaller scale and was renamed Bugs Bunny High Sea Adventure in 2016. Originally opened as the Santa Maria in 1986.

Satellite Rides
1967-1973
Spinning rides where riders would sit in pairs on the edge of a rotating disc, then the ride would spin and raise up at an angle of about 45 degrees.

Shake, Rattle and Roll
2004-2010
Scrambler ride in the old Chevy Show building. The ride had three arms coming off a central hub and each arm had four cars that would spin at a different rate than the arms themselves, "scrambling" the riders. Loud music would play as the ride would spin and lights would flash to heighten the discombobulation.

Shirt Tales
1984-1985
Walk around characters based off Hallmark's Shirt Tales cartoon and greeting card line. There were five animals; a tiger, raccoon, panda, possum, and an orangutan. Each had a different message on their shirt like *Top Banana* or *Hug Me*. Shirt Tales the cartoon was cancelled in 1984 and they stayed one more year at SFOG, overlapping the arrival of Bugs Bunny and friends by a year.

Ship Shape Theatre
1980-1985
Pirate themed theater located in Jolly Roger's Island that hosted a pirate themed comedy show. It was renamed and rethemed as Graffiti's in 1986.

Showcase Theatre
1987-1993
Located in the U.S.A. Section, the Showcase Theatre was a renamed and redecorated Looney Tunes Theatre. Showcase Theatre was itself renamed the Remember When Drive-In Theatre in 1994 As the Showcase Theatre, the exterior had a fountain that started at the roofline and poured into a pool at the base of the front wall. The interior of the theatre has remained similar over the years, with the show inside changing every few years.

Six Flags Railroad
1967-Current
Traditional looking trains that ride guests around the park. The engines used to run on steam, but they have been retrofitted to run on diesel fuel. There are two stations guests may board the train: Marthasville Station in Peachtree Square and Rabun Gap in the French Section.

Skull Island
2005-2013
Original water park style play area in the park. Themed with pirates and buried treasure, it was a play fort style attraction. It was absorbed into Hurricane Harbor in 2014 and rethemed to fit the new water park aesthetics.

Sky Buckets
1968-Current
Cable cars that connect the Peachtree Square and the Lickskillet sections of the park. Guests will reach a height of 70 feet as they glide over the park in the bucket-like cars. At one time, there were two sets of sky buckets that crisscrossed the park, with the first set of cable cars, the Astro Lift, lasting from 1967-1981.

Sky Coaster
2010-Current
Large swing ride that includes an additional cost not included with park admission. 180 foot arch with a swinging platform for guests to lie down suspended within the arch. The platform is pulled back and riders swing out over the same lake that houses the Great American Scream Machine. It opened in 1996 as Feerless Freep's Daredevil Dive but changed its name in 2010 to Sky Coaster when the Dare Devil Dive roller coaster opened.

Sky Hook
1969-1977
Ride designed to show the surrounding landscape, not so much a thrill ride. The structure of the ride looked like a large Y and had an oval shaped pod that hung from each branch. While one was one the ground, the other would be at the top. The ride had a recording in the pod describing what the guests would see from the top of the attraction. This ride was located in the U.S.A. Section.

SkyScreamer
2013-Current
The park's tallest ride at a height of 242 feet, this giant swing ride rotates riders at 43 miles per hour. Riders load into their swings on the ground and then the central gondola is raised to the top of the pole and begins to spin, forcing the swings out and giving riders a view of the rear of the park and the Atlanta skyline.

Sol Caliente
1974-1984
Kiddie sized Ferris Wheel themed after the sun, with decorations fitting in with the Spanish/Mexican theme. It was rethemed and renamed Elmer Fudd's Fewwis Wheel to fit in with the new Looney Tunes Section.

Southern Star Amphitheater
1986-2013
Concert venue that was built upon a large parking lot in the rear of the park that is now the location of Hurricane Harbor. Before the amphitheater was built, concerts were held on the lot and guests had to stand on the hard asphalt to see concerts. The amphitheater was built and had a combination of 2,000 fixed seats and a grass berm behind the seats for general admission capacity of 18,000 for a total capacity of 20,000. All kinds of performers played the amphitheater over the years. As newer concert venues were built in metro Atlanta, the demand for the Southern Star Amphitheater declined and was eventually replaced by the water park, Skull Island.

Spanish Section
1967-2015
One of the original sections of the park, inspired by the brief section of Georgia that was under Spanish rule. The focus of this section was Castile DeSoto. Early in the life of the park, the staff who worked in the Spanish Section would dress in Spanish Conquistador costumes. Bugs Bunny and his friends slowly pushed the Spanish Section out, rendering the area almost unrecognizable today.

Speedy Gonzales Speed Boats
2016-Current
Flat spinning attraction with speedboat ride vehicles for the children to ride in. The boats spin around a central hub with no change in height.

Spindle Top
1968-1979
Spinning ride that would stick riders to the outside wall with centrifugal force and then the floor below would drop out from under their feet.

Splashwater Falls
1986-Current
Large flume ride where the boats go up a hill and then drop 50 feet soaking the people in the front and rear of the boats. Guests also stand on the bridge over the ride to be splashed as well.

Superman: Tower of Power
2016-Current
Tower drop ride with consisting of a pole with a ride vehicle that will raise slowly up the pole and then drop. Designed for riders too big for Tweety's Tweehouse and too small for Acrophobia.

Superman: Ultimate Flight
2002-Current
Steel flying roller coaster with a top speed of 51 mph and maximum height of 106 feet. The ride trains hang from the rail instead of riding on it and the riders themselves hang parallel to the track, facing the ground for a majority of the ride. The coaster is designed to simulate flying as if guests were Superman.

Swing Seville
1994-2015
Kiddie sized swing ride for the little riders who weren't big enough for the other swings rides throughout the park. It opened as Tweety's Swings in 1985 and was renamed Swing Seville in 1994. When the area was renamed and rethemed in 2016, Swing Seville was removed.

T

Tales of the Okefenokee
1967-1980
Uncle Remus themed ride through boat attraction. It opened with the park in 1967 and the entire ride was redone for 1968 by Sid and Marty Kroft, with the same Uncle Remus theming. The ride closed in 1980 and was completely rethemed into Monster Plantation while keeping the same boat layout. Disneyland would later use the Uncle Remus theme for their own water ride in 1989 with Splash Mountain.

Tank Tag
1992-1994
Remote control attraction where guests would control miniature tanks that would fire at each other and targets in the arena.

The Great American Force
1986-1986
Carnival style ride brought in for a few months at the end of 1986 after Mo-Mo the Monster was removed after being struck by lightning. The ride would have riders stand against a circular cage while the ride would spin fast, using centrifugal force to push the guests up against the wall. While spinning, the ride would start to tilt, allowing guests to be looking down at the other passengers as they spun, only being held up in the air by centrifugal force.

The Great Six Flags Air Racer
1984-2000
Airplane ride with twelve open cockpit fiberglass biplanes that would raise up and spin around a large tower, giving guests glimpses of the park and the skyline of Atlanta in the distance. This ride was partially removed in 2000. The planes and cables were removed, but the 125 foot tall pole remained and became Acrophobia.

The Joker Funhouse Coaster
2016-Current
Steel roller coaster designed for the smaller guests of the park. It has a top speed of 30 mph and is 28 feet tall. The coaster winds around and through the Joker's Funhouse, the central piece of the DC Super Friends area. Originally opened in 2004 as the Wile E. Coyote Canyon Blaster, was repainted and renamed The Joker Funhouse Coaster in 2016.

The Joker: Chaos Coaster
2015-Current
Circular coaster ride where riders face each other and the ride train rocks back and forth on the 72 foot tall loop track before making the complete loop and turning riders upside down. Similar rider sensation to the retired Looping Starship.

Thomas Town
2008-2010
Children's area themed after Thomas the Tank Engine. The main attraction was a miniature train ride that was pulled by Thomas himself. There was also a Thomas themed play area where children could climb over and through Thomas' friends. This area was renamed Whistlestop Park in 2011.

Thunder River
1982-Current
River rapids ride where guests shoot the rapids and bounce off items throughout the river route. To ensure that everyone is properly wet, there is a waterfall at the end for the boats to go under. Opened in 1982.

Tondee's Tavern Restaurant
1967-2007
One of the original restaurants in the park, located in the British Section that was designed to help the area look like a quaint English town. The irony in the restaurant's name in the British Section is that Tondee's Tavern was named after the bar in Savannah, GA of the same name. The original Tondee's Tavern was the meeting place for the American Revolutionaries against the British in the late 18th century. The first government for the state of Georgia was drafted in Tondee's Tavern, making it an odd name for the British Section. In 2008, Tondee's Tavern became Johnny Rockets.

Toro Toro
1994-2015
Circular flat kiddie ride with ride vehicles shaped like bulls that rotated around a central hub.

Treasure Chest Arcade
1992-1994
Video arcade located in the Jolly Rodger Section with pirate theming and name, but regular games on the inside.

Tsunami Surge
2014-Current
Water ride in Hurricane Harbor in which four riders ride a float down an enclosed tube into a whirlpool bowl that swishes the raft around before depositing guests into the pool. This attraction opened in 2014.

Tweety's Clubhouse
2001-2014
A tower-style drop ride for the little riders. Kids sit on a bench that slowly raises up on a tree with Tweety Bird at the top. Once it reaches a height of 20 feet, Tweety swings a mallet at the bench and it shakes and rattles as it falls. This process is repeated a few times to complete the ride. Originally opened as Tweety's Clubhouse in 2001 and was renamed Tweety's Tweehouse in 2015.

Tweety's Swings
1985-1993
When the Looney Tunes area opened in 1985, Tweety's Swings opened as an alternative for the guests who were too young or small to ride the larger swing rides in the park. This ride was renamed Swing Seville in 1994.

Tweety's Tweehouse
2015-Current
A tower-style drop ride for the little riders. Kids sit on a bench that slowly raises up on a tree with Tweety Bird at the top. Once it reaches a height of 20 feet, Tweety swings a mallet at the bench and it shakes and rattles as it falls. This process is repeated a few times to complete the ride. Originally opened as Tweety's Clubhouse in 2001 and was renamed Tweety's Tweehouse in 2015.

Twisted Cyclone
2018-Current
Hybrid steel and wooden coaster, replacing the Georgia Cyclone. Using part of the same track as the Georgia Cyclone, the coaster keeps the same height and speed (95ft and 50 mph), but adds three inversions. The ride vehicles are modeled after 1960s sports convertibles.

Ultrazone
1995-1996
Laser tag attraction located inside a building in the U.S.A. Section where groups of guests were fitted with sensors and given rifles that would fire lasers. The attraction was located in a dark building with barriers to hide behind and artificial smoke to see the lasers as they shot through the air. The sensors would register the amount of hits and the teams with the most successful shots would win.

Up, Up & Away
2004-Current
Swing-style ride with hot air balloon hanging basket styled ride cars that raise guests up to twelve feet in the air as they spin around the central hub.

U.S.A. Section
1967-Current
One of the original sections in the park, often referred to the modern section early in the park's history. In the early 1990's the area was rethemed to a 1950's aesthetic. Instead of constantly trying to stay modern, the area was now full of neon, retro theming, and a drive-in theater.

U.S.A. Theatre
1998-2003
Theater with a screen that went 180 degrees around the audience and arched overhead as well. It would show point of view films to make viewers feel like they were actually participating in the films (riding roller coasters, driving speeding cars, etc.), not just watching a movie. The screen was removed and the U.S.A. Theatre ended as a performing arts venue. It was located in the U.S.A. Section and was previously named the Plymouth Theatre. When the sponsorship by Plymouth ended, it was renamed the U.S.A. Theatre.

Viper
1995-2001
Steel loop roller coaster that was a relatively short ride. The trains would launch from the station, shoot through the loop, go up a bit of track, and do the loop in reverse back into the station. It had a top speed of 57 mph and was 138 feet tall.

Watermelon Waterloo
1968-Closed (Undetermined)
Watermelon store that was located in the French Section. Guests were able to purchase chilled wedges of watermelon for snacks.

Wheel Burrow
1968-1970
Double Ferris Wheel that consisted of two wheels separated by an axis so the wheels could not only spin in the traditional perpendicular to the ground manner, but could rotate the wheels were parallel to the ground, with one being stuck far up in the air while the other is spinning flat near the ground. This ride was in the Lickskillet Section and was replaced by the Drunken Barrels.

Wheelie
1977-2012
The ride would start with the wheel parallel to the ground and the ride vehicles hanging around the rim. As the ride would start to spin, the ride vehicles would start to swing out a little bit, then the main wheel in the center would start to tilt until it was almost perpendicular to the ground with the guests still spinning. It originally opened in the U.S.A. Section and in 1985, the ride was moved to the former site of the Drunken Barrels in the Lickskillet Section. It was removed for construction of SkyScreamer.

Whistlestop Park
2011-2015
Train themed area that replaced Thomas Town after the official licensed theming was removed. The train was removed after a year, but the entire train themed section held on until 2015 when the playground was relocated to Bugs Bunny Boomtown and the area itself was closed off.

Wilie E Coyote Canyon Blaster
2004-2015

Steel roller coaster designed for the smaller guests of the park. It has a top speed of 30 mph and is 28 feet tall. The coaster winds around and through the Joker's Funhouse, the central piece of the DC Super Friends area. Originally opened in 2004 as the Wile E. Coyote Canyon Blaster, was repainted and renamed The Joker Funhouse Coaster in 2016.

Wonder Woman Flight School
2016-Current

Flying scooter ride for kids with a Wonder Woman theme. Similar to a traditional swing ride, but the ride vehicles had rudders on the back, allowing guests some control over their path while being spun.

Yahoola Hooler
1969-1972
Steel junior coaster that was built for the smaller riders to enjoy as their more adult family members enjoyed the Dahlonega Mine Train. The Mini Mine Train track looped through the track for the Dahlonega Mine Train and shared the same early gold rush theming. It originally opened as the Yahoola Hooler in 1969 and was renamed the Mini Mine Train in 1973. It had a top speed of 20 mph and was 20 feet tall.

Yosemite Sam Playfort
1985-2015
The playfort rethemed the Pac-Man Playfort, keeping many of the attractions and giving them a Looney Tunes name. The ball pit, pipeline crawl, and hanging bop bags remained. The bop bags were turned into carrots and renamed the Carrot Patch. This area remained a Looney Tunes themed area until 2016, when DC Comics characters moved in.

Yosemite Sam's Wacky Wagons
2016-Current
Child-size Ferris wheel with cabins in the shape of Conestoga wagons. Originally opened as Sol Caliente in 1974. It was renamed the Elmer Fudd's Fewwis Wheel in 1985 and renamed the Fiesta Wheel in 1994. It was again renamed and rethemed in 2016 as Yosemite Sam's Wacky Wagons.

Z

Z-Force
1988-1991
Blue and white steel roller coaster that was the world's only hairpin drop roller coaster. It was also the only space dive coaster to ever be built. The quick dives and climbs would produce a freefall feeling for the riders, producing up to 3-Gs of force. It had a top speed of 35 mph and was 86 feet tall.

Made in the USA
Las Vegas, NV
14 December 2021